SELF-ASSESSMENT

REALITY-BASED LEADERSHIP

CY WAKEMAN

From *The New York Times* Best-Selling Author of
The Reality-Based Rules of the Workplace

WILEY

Instructions

Below you will find twenty-four statements that describe dimensions of leadership behavior. Read each statement carefully and then circle the number that best reflects the degree to which you agree or disagree with that statement. Every statement must have a rating.

1 = Completely Disagree

2 = Mostly Disagree

3 = Somewhat Disagree

4 = Somewhat Agree

5 = Mostly Agree

6 = Completely Agree

1. The difference between success and failure is commitment.

    1   2   3   4   5   6

2. Decision-makers should take my opinion into account when making their decisions.

    1   2   3   4   5   6

3. Employees need to be given ample time to buy in to changes in the organization.

    1   2   3   4   5   6

4. I regularly participate in development experiences that are not funded by or arranged by my organization.

    1   2   3   4   5   6

5. Most employees have more influence on their supervisors than they think they do.

    1   2   3   4   5   6

1 = Completely Disagree   4 = Somewhat Agree

2 = Mostly Disagree   5 = Mostly Agree

3 = Somewhat Disagree   6 = Completely Agree

6. I consider myself active in social networking.

   1   2   3   4   5   6

7. When I consider issues that have prevented me from achieving positive results, I regularly identify things I could have done differently to change the outcome.

   1   2   3   4   5   6

8. My manager should provide me all the information and direction I need to do my job.

   1   2   3   4   5   6

9. I love receiving suggestions for how to do my job better.

   1   2   3   4   5   6

10. An individual is responsible for learning what he or she needs to be successful.

   1   2   3   4   5   6

11. Co-workers owe it to each other to offer suggestions for improvement.

   1   2   3   4   5   6

12. Success or failure often depends on how many obstacles there are in the way (that is, resource constraints, customer expectations, etc.).

   1   2   3   4   5   6

13. Doing more than what's expected is the key to getting ahead in life.

   1   2   3   4   5   6

14. Taking credit and accepting blame are equally important.

   1   2   3   4   5   6

1 = Completely Disagree   4 = Somewhat Agree

2 = Mostly Disagree   5 = Mostly Agree

3 = Somewhat Disagree   6 = Completely Agree

15. The main difference between success and failure is luck.

    1   2   3   4   5   6

16. My co-workers' behavior prevents me from doing my best work.

    1   2   3   4   5   6

17. When an employee has a problem, his or her manager should try to fix it.

    1   2   3   4   5   6

18. Most of what happens at work is out of my control.

    1   2   3   4   5   6

19. My past failures have prepared me to succeed in the future.

    1   2   3   4   5   6

20. It is acceptable for an employee's personal life to affect his or her performance at work.

    1   2   3   4   5   6

21. A person's ability to deal with change is determined by his or her personality and is therefore difficult to influence.

    1   2   3   4   5   6

22. Employees should be consulted on decisions that are going to affect them.

    1   2   3   4   5   6

23. It is inevitable to be in a bad mood at work some days.

    1   2   3   4   5   6

24. When I am frustrated, it is due to situations or circumstances outside my control.

    1   2   3   4   5   6

Reality-Based Leadership Profile Scoring

Instructions

1. Transfer the answers (numbers) you gave for each item to the scoring framework below. Note that the items are not in sequential order.

2. Add the numbers in each column and write the sum in the space provided.

Column A

1. _____

4. _____

5. _____

6. _____

7. _____

9. _____

10. _____

11. _____

13. _____

14. _____

19. _____

Column B

2. _____

3. _____

8. _____

12. _____

15. _____

16. _____

17. _____

18. _____

20. _____

21. _____

22. _____

23. _____

24. _____

SUM Column A: _____   SUM Column B: _____

Reality-based leaders have a score in Column A of 50 or higher and a score in Column B of 25 or less. If your score is different, don't despair. The Reality-Based Leadership Workshop is for you! If you are in alignment, that is good news.

In the Reality-Based Leadership Workshop, we will discuss non-conventional leadership practices that typically resonate with leaders and help them improve their business results. You will learn why some common approaches to the statements in this assessment actually create drama and hinder results. The Reality-Based Leadership Workshop will help you live from a more accountable context and be an example for others.

Discover more at www.wiley.com

WILEY

ISBN 978-1-118-54046-6